Loom Knit Garter Slip Chain Patterns

By Scarlett Royale

Loom Knit Garter Slip Chain Patterns
By
Scarlett Royale

Table Of Content:
Introduction: 3
Terminology: 4-8
Ear Warmer: 9
Hat: 10-12
Cowl: 13
Fingerless Gloves: 14-15
Bracelet: 16
Boot Cuffs: 17
Leg Warmers: 18
Booties: 19-21
Cell Phone Case: 22
Hooded Capelet: 23-24

Introduction

The garter slip chain is a set of stitch patterns, brought together, to create depth and texture. The garter stitch, known for being the horizontal like rib stitch. The slip, where you skip a row, and slip the stitch over on the next row, creating a longer looking stitch. The chain, which is based on a crochet technique, where you chain a ladder, and weave it later to look like a braid. This is why I call this book the "Garter Slip Chain".

When I originally worked up a strip of this design, I had a flood of ideas on how to incorporate it into a multitude of projects. Consider this book a guide, to get you started on you own project, using the garter slip chain. While the chain part may be difficult to grasp at first, once you have it, it will be a wonderful thing to use over and over, to create a variety of projects.

This book will provide you with written, picture, and video tutorial to help you get on your way to creating these classic style patterns. So no matter how you learn, you should be able to work up these patterns, but if you have any questions, please feel free to contact me and ask.

Happy Looming!!!! Video Tutorial for Basic Band: https://youtu.be/IIE_jQI0dBk

Terminology

CO: Cast On: Process of E-Wrapping all the pegs

EW: E-Wrap: Process of wrapping the working yarn behind the peg, then around to the front and back again, toss the bottom loop over the top.

P: Purl: Process of pulling the working yarn through the bottom to the top of the stitch, take original stitch off, and place the new stitch on the loom.

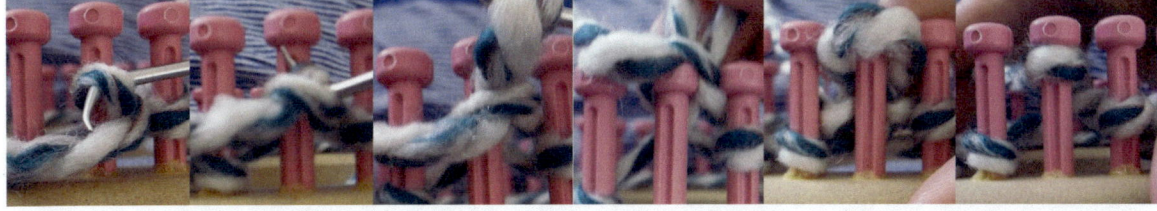

K: Flat Knit: Process of tossing the bottom loop over the top working yarn, make sure to pull the bottom stitch, you just tossed over into the middle of the loom before releasing, this allows the stitch you just made to be looser.

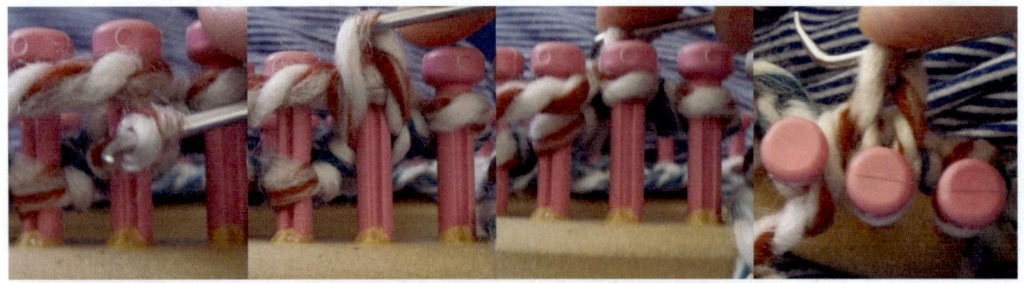

SK: Skip: Process of taking the working yarn behind the peg, and moving to the next peg.

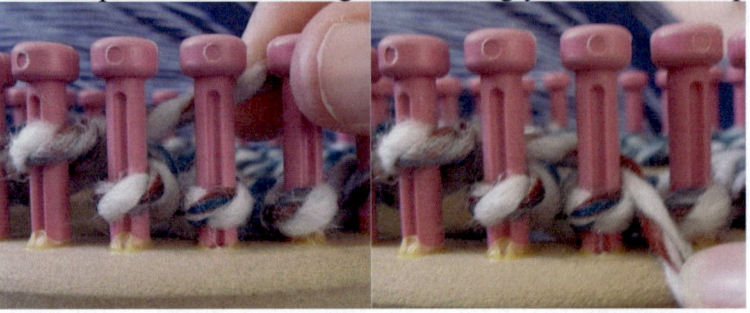

EWCH D-> BOLB: E-Wrap Chain Decrease Right Bring Original Loop Back: E-Wrap Chain by E-Wrapping the same peg however many times. Then decrease by moving that last chain right, to the next peg, and toss the bottom loop over. Then bring the original loop back, on the empty peg you just made by decreasing.

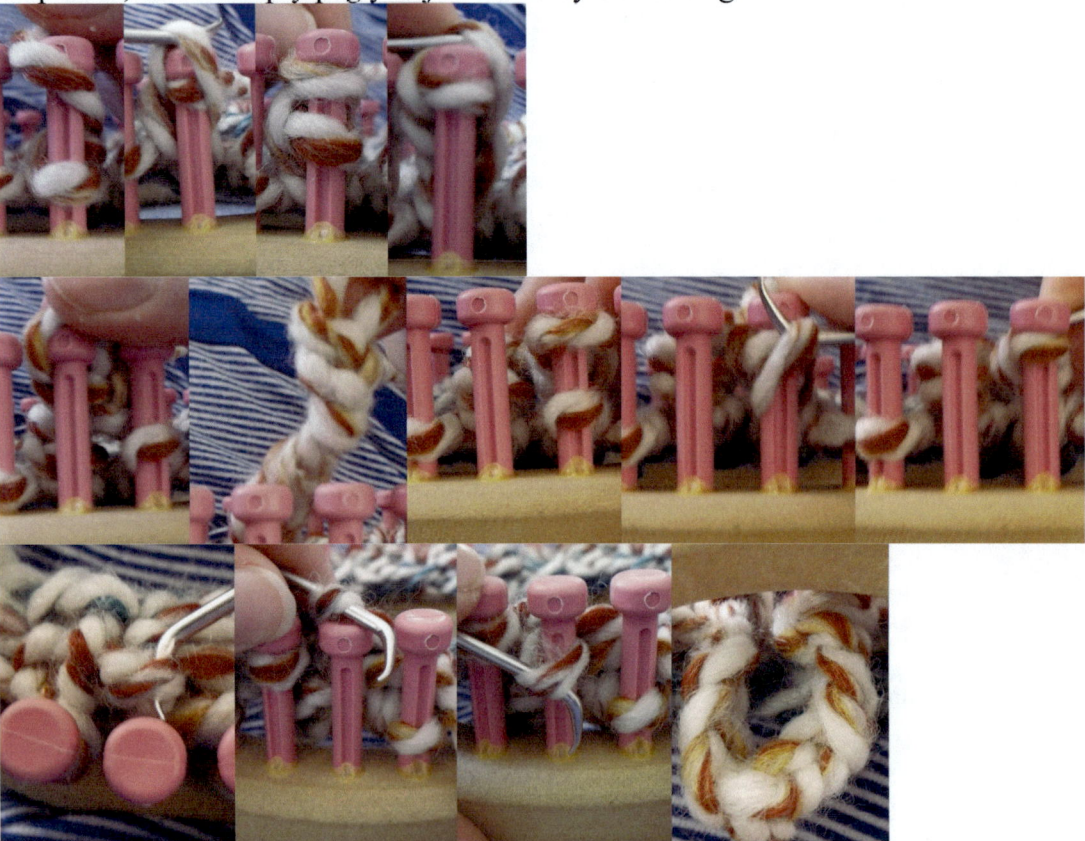

WT: Wrap and Turn: Process of taking the working yarn, and wrapping it behind the next un-worked peg, and around to the front, this allows you to start working the other direction.

4

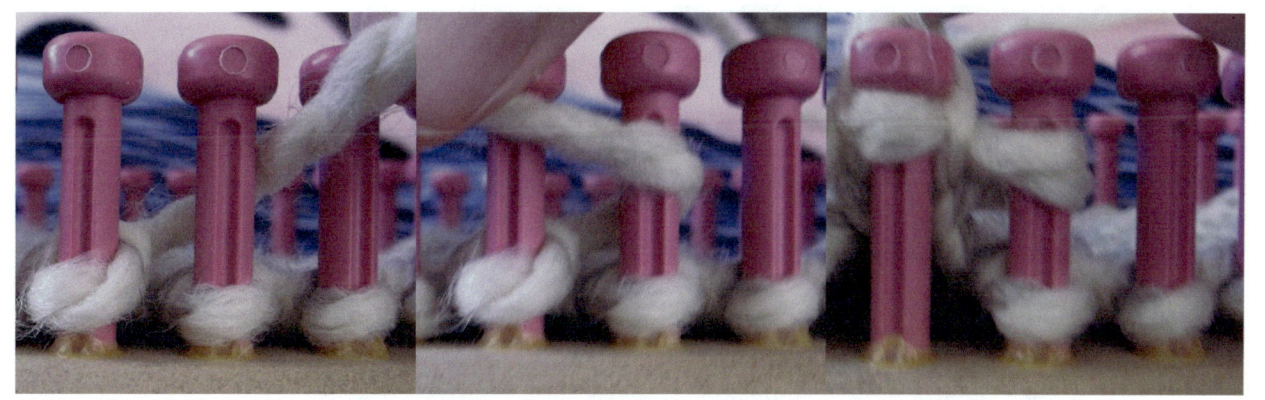

COF: Cast Off: E-Wrap pegs 1 and 2, place stitch 2 on peg 1, and toss the bottom loop over. Now move the stitch over to fill the gap. Now E-Wrap the 2nd peg, then move loop 2 to peg 1 and toss the bottom loop over. Move the stitch over to fill the gap. Repeat from the move to fill the gap.

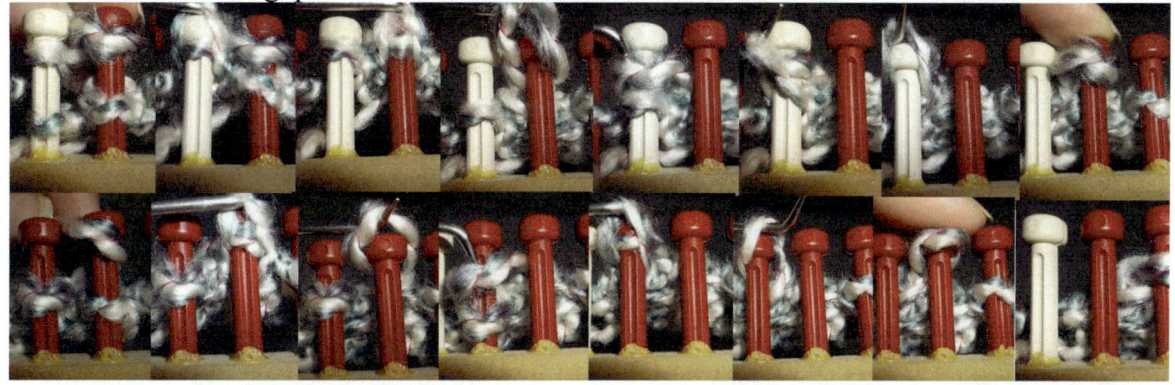

KBO: Kitchener Bind Off: The Process of moving half of the stitches, to the other half evenly, then begin this weaving technique. Send the needle through the bottom stitch, like a knit, from the top. Then send the needle through the top stitch, like a knit, though the top. Then move to the next peg, send the needle through the top loop, like a purl, from the bottom. Then go back to the 1st peg, and send the needle through the bottom stitch, like a purl, through the bottom of the stitch. Now go back to the next peg, and send the needle through the bottom stitch, like a knit. This gets you started with the pattern. Start following from the needle going through the top stitch, like a knit.

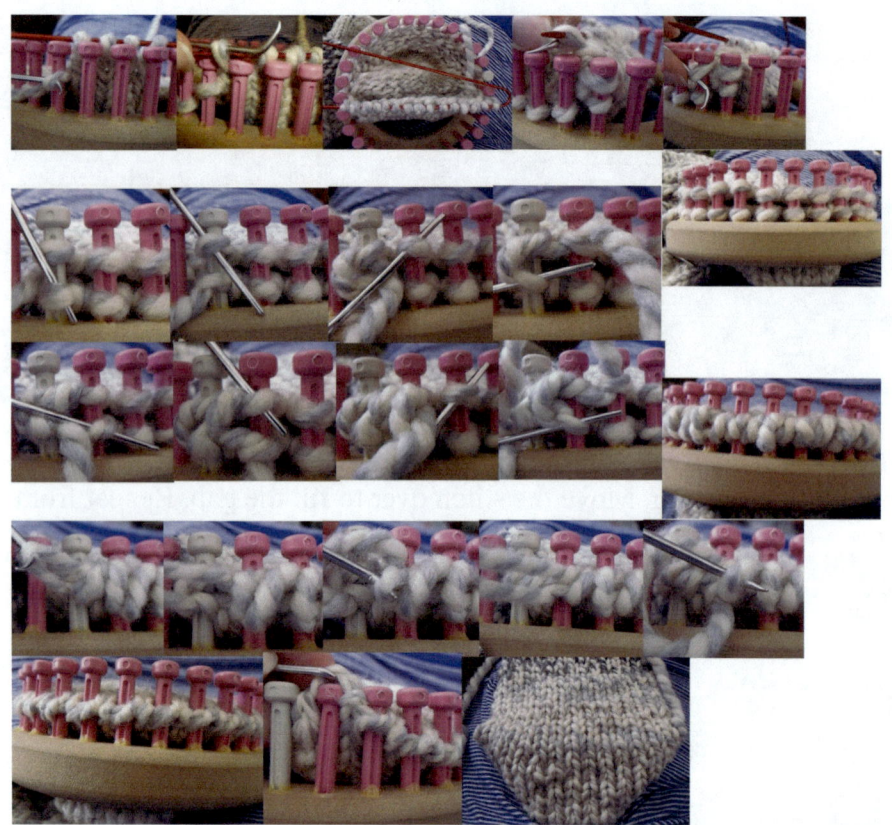

DDDSCOF: Double Decrease Draw String Cast Off: Process off EW the 1st peg, move to the next peg, and toss the bottom loop over. Then go to the next peg, EW, move to the next peg, and toss the bottom loop over. Do this to all the pegs, this halves your stitches. Then do the same process as above, but instead of following the pegs through the process, you are following the stitches that exist on the pegs. You will EW the next peg with a stitch, then move to the next peg with a stitch, and toss the bottom loop over. Do this to all the pegs with stitches. This will half your stitches again. Now send a needle through all the stitches left, take the stitches off, and draw string the stitches together.

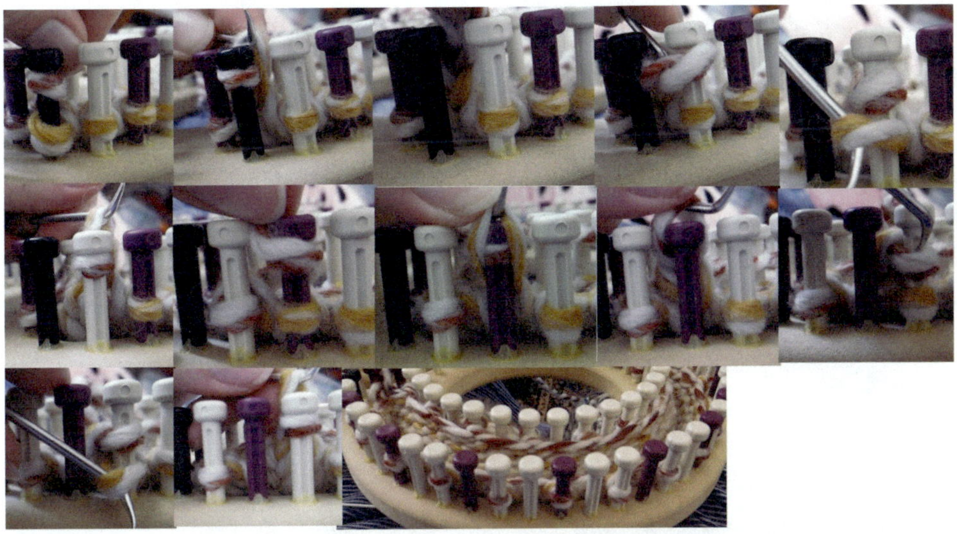

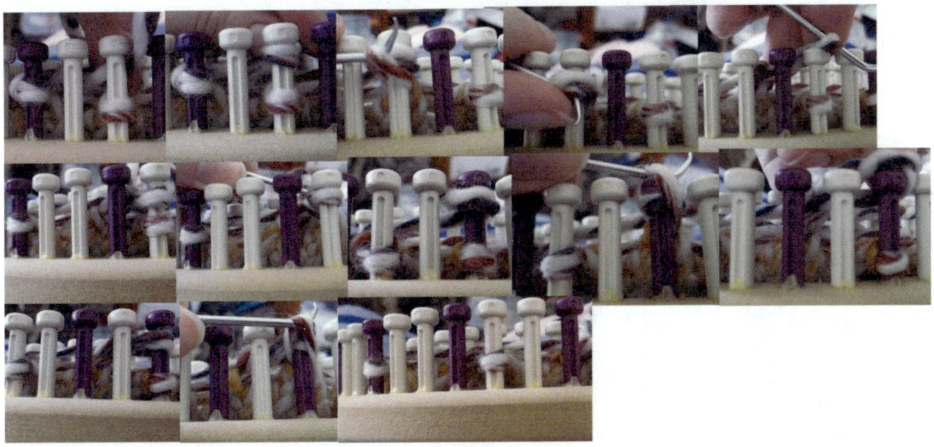

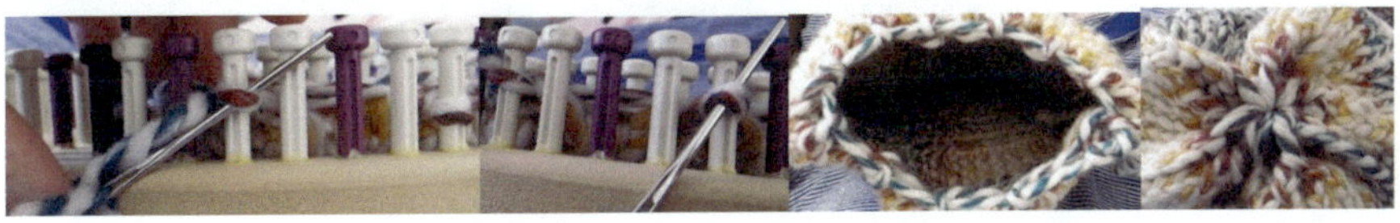

WCO: Weave In Cast On: 
Start with the right side of the panel facing out, shove 1 end of the panel into the center of the loom. Send the crochet hook through the bridge between the 2 ridges at the top edge of your panel, grab the working yarn and pull through the bridge, place the loop on the peg. Continue the process of pulling the working yarn through the bridge between each secion, doing this all the way around till the top edge of the panel is attached to the loom.

Braid the Chain

Ear Warmer

Video Tutorial: https://youtu.be/IIE_jQI0dBk

Items:
18 peg 1/2" Gauge CinDwood Loom
Looming Hook
Crafters Needle
1 Skein of Lions Brand Thick and Quick Wool Ease
Measuring Tape

Terms:
EW: E-Wrap
CO: Cast On
K: Flat Knit
P: Purl
SK: Skip
EWCH D-> BOLB: E-Wrap Chain, Decrease to the Right, Bring Original Loop Back on Empty Peg.
COF: Cast Off

EWCO 18 pegs
Row 1: EW4, P1, EW2, P1, EW2, P1, EW2, P1, EW4
Row 2: P4, P1, Sk2, P1, EW2, P1, Sk2, P1, P4
Row 3: K4, P1, EW2, P1, EW2, P1, EW2, P1, K4
Row 4: P4, P1, Sk2, P1, EWCH10 D-> BOLB, P1, Sk2, P1, P4
Row 5: K4, P1, EW2, P1, EW2, P1, EW2, P1, K4
Follow Rows 2-5 24 times, or to the length you desire to fit to a particular size head.
COF

Braid your chain, then sew ends together, while sewing in your end chain. You're Done!!!!

Hat

Video Tutorial Band: https://youtu.be/IIE_jQI0dBk
Video Tutorial Hat: https://youtu.be/ZQTETZBNz08

Items:
S-Loom 1/2" Gauge CinDwood Loom with Wedge
Looming Hook
Crochet Hook (Size H)
Crafters Needle
1 Skein of Lions Brand Thick and Quick Wool Ease
Measuring Tape

Terms:
EW: E-Wrap
CO: Cast On
WCO: Weave In Cast On
K: Flat Knit
P: Purl
SK: Skip
EWCH D-> BOLB: E-Wrap Chain, Decrease to the Right, Bring Original Loop Back on Empty Peg
DDDSCOF: Double Decrease Draw String Cast Off

EWCO 18 pegs
Row 1: EW4, P1, EW2, P1, EW2, P1, EW2, P1, EW4
Row 2: P4, P1, Sk2, P1, EW2, P1, Sk2, P1, P4

Row 3: K4, P1, EW2, P1, EW2, P1, EW2, P1, K4
Row 4: P4, P1, Sk2, P1, EWCH10 D-> BOLB, P1, Sk2, P1, P4
Row 5: K4, P1, EW2, P1, EW2, P1, EW2, P1, K4
Follow Rows 2-5 24 times, or to the length you desire to fit to a particular size head.
COF

Braid your chain, then sew ends together while sewing in your end chain.

For Adult Hat
WCO 52 pegs
Row 1-10: EW

DDDSCOF

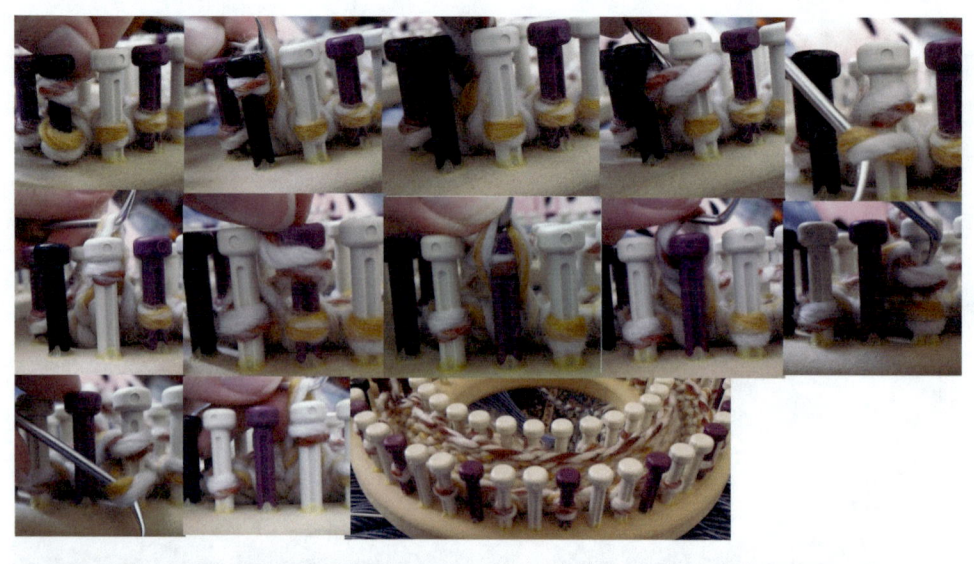

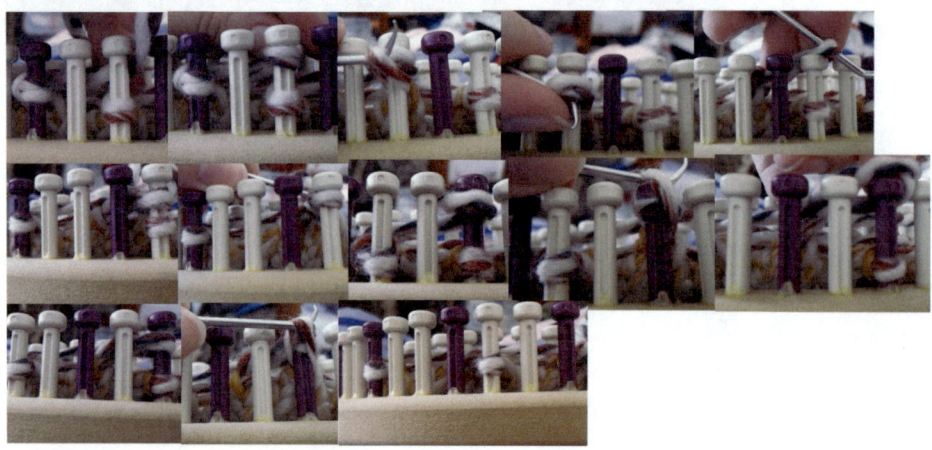

To customize your hat to a smaller or larger size, follow the ear warmer to the length you need, count your ridges, then WCO to your universal loom. Large Adult EW15 rows, Child EW 8rows, after WCO.
You're Done!!!

Cowl

Video Tutorial: https://youtu.be/HZwUTPfTeEA

Items:
30 peg 1/2" Gauge CinDwood Loom
Looming Hook
Crafters Needle
2 Skeins of Lions Brand Thick and Quick Wool Ease

Terms:
EW: E-Wrap
CO: Cast On
K: Flat Knit
P: Purl
SK: Skip
EWCH D-> BOLB: E-Wrap Chain, Decrease to the Right, Bring Original Loop Back on Empty Peg
COF: Cast Off

EWCO 30 pegs circularly
Row 1: EW3, P1, EW2, P1, EW2, P1, EW2, P1, EW4, P1, EW2, P1, EW2, P1, EW2, P1, EW3
Row 2: P3, P1, Sk2, P1, EW2, P1, Sk2, P1, P4, P1, Sk2, P1, EW2, P1, Sk2, P1, P3
Row 3: K3, P1, EW2, P1, EW2, P1, EW2, P1, K4, P1, EW2, P1, EW2, P1, EW2, P1, K3
Row 4: P3, P1, Sk2, P1, EWCH10 D-> BOLB, P1, Sk2, P1, P4, P1, Sk2, P1, EWCH10 D-> BOLB, P1, Sk2, P1, P3
Row 5: K3, P1, EW2, P1, EW2, P1, EW2, P1, K4, P1, EW2, P1, EW2, P1, EW2, P1, K3
Repeat rows 2-5 51 more times.
COF
Weave your chains into a braid, sew ends together, and you're done!!!

Fingerless Gloves

Video Tutorial: https://youtu.be/IIE_jQI0dBk

Items:
30peg 1/2" gauge CinDwood Loom
Looming Hook
Crafters Needle
2 Skein of Lions Brand Thick and Quick Wool Ease Yarn
Measuring Tape

Terms:
EW: E-Wrap
CO: Cast On
K: Flat Knit
P: Purl
SK: Skip
EWCH D-> BOLB: E-Wrap Chain, Decrease to the Right, Bring Original Loop Back on Empty Peg
COF: Cast Off

EWCO 22
Row 1: EW6, P1, EW2, P1, EW2, P1, EW2, P1, EW6
Row 2: P6, P1, Sk2, P1, EW2, P1, Sk2, P1, P6
Row 3: K6, P1, EW2, P1, EW2, P1, EW2, P1, K6
Row 4: P6, P1, Sk2, P1, EWCH10 D-> BOLB, P1, Sk2, P1, P6
Row 5: K6, P1, EW2, P1, EW2, P1, EW2, P1, K6
Follow Rows 2-5 12 times, COF. Or however long it needs to be to go around the wrist of the person you are making it for.

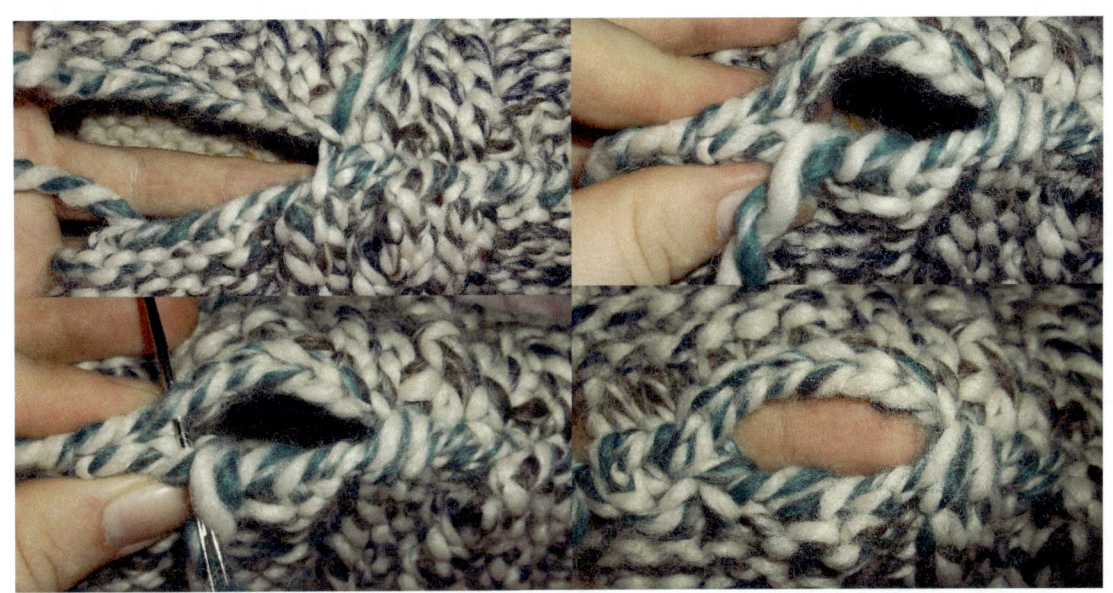

Sew up band until you get to the 2nd slip section, stop, weave in your needle on one side into half of the garter section, then sew the other half of the garter section to finish the gloves. Repeat on both gloves. The weave section prevents for lots of cutting and tying off, while making an opening for your thumbs. You're Done!!!

Bracelet

Video Tutorial: https://youtu.be/mHvKvaGx28I

Items:
1/4" gauge CinDwood Loom
Looming Hook
Crochet Hook
Crafters Needle
Rhinestone Button
Size 3 to 4 Metallic Yarn 40 to 50yds worth
Measuring Tape

Terms:
EW: E-Wrap
CO: Cast On
K: Flat Knit
P: Purl
SK: Skip
EWCH D-> BOLB: E-Wrap Chain, Decrease to the Right, Bring Original Loop Back on Empty Peg
COF: Cast Off

EWCO 18 pegs
Row 1: EW4, P1, EW2, P1, EW2, P1, EW2, P1, EW4
Row 2: P4, P1, Sk2, P1, EW2, P1, Sk2, P1, P4
Row 3: K4, P1, EW2, P1, EW2, P1, EW2, P1, K4
Row 4: P4, P1, Sk2, P1, EWCH10 D-> BOLB, P1, Sk2, P1, P4
Row 5: K4, P1, EW2, P1, EW2, P1, EW2, P1, K4
Follow Rows 2-5 however many times to get the length you want for the wrist, measure out. The bracelet will stretch some.
COF
Weave your chains into a braid, sew ends together, sew on button, and hook last chain over button. You're Done!!!

Boot Cuffs

Video Tutorial: https://youtu.be/IIE_jQI0dBk

Items:
18peg 1/2" gauge CinDwood Loom
Looming Hook
Crafters Needle
1 Skein of Lions Brand Thick and Quick Wool Ease Yarn
Measuring Tape

Terms:
EW: E-Wrap
CO: Cast On
K: Flat Knit
P: Purl
SK: Skip
EWCH D-> BOLB: E-Wrap Chain, Decrease to the Right, Bring Original Loop Back on Empty Peg
COF: Cast Off

EWCO 18 pegs
Row 1: EW4, P1, EW2, P1, EW2, P1, EW2, P1, EW4
Row 2: P4, P1, Sk2, P1, EW2, P1, Sk2, P1, P4
Row 3: K4, P1, EW2, P1, EW2, P1, EW2, P1, K4
Row 4: P4, P1, Sk2, P1, EWCH10 D-> BOLB, P1, Sk2, P1, P4
Row 5: K4, P1, EW2, P1, EW2, P1, EW2, P1, K4
Follow Rows 2-5 however many times to get the length you want for the calf or ankle, measure out. The band will stretch some. I did 15 times.
COF

Weave chain into braid, sew ends together attaching your last chain in the middle, when seaming the ends together. You're Done!!

Leg Warmers

Video Tutorial: https://youtu.be/HZwUTPfTeEA

Items:
30 peg 1/2" Gauge CinDwood Loom
Looming Hook
Crafters Needle
2 Skeins of Lions Brand Thick and Quick Wool Ease
Measuring Tape

Terms:
EW: E-Wrap
CO: Cast On
K: Flat Knit
P: Purl
SK: Skip
EWCH D-> BOLB: E-Wrap Chain, Decrease to the Right, Bring Original Loop Back on Empty Peg
COF: Cast Off

EWCO 30 pegs circularly
Row 1: EW3, P1, EW2, P1, EW2, P1, EW2, P1, EW4, P1, EW2, P1, EW2, P1, EW2, P1, EW3
Row 2: P3, P1, Sk2, P1, EW2, P1, Sk2, P1, P4, P1, Sk2, P1, EW2, P1, Sk2, P1, P3
Row 3: K3, P1, EW2, P1, EW2, P1, EW2, P1, K4, P1, EW2, P1, EW2, P1, EW2, P1, K3
Row 4: P3, P1, Sk2, P1, EWCH10 D-> BOLB, P1, Sk2, P1, P4, P1, Sk2, P1, EWCH10 D-> BOLB, P1, Sk2, P1, P3
Row 5: K3, P1, EW2, P1, EW2, P1, EW2, P1, K4, P1, EW2, P1, EW2, P1, EW2, P1, K3
Repeat rows 2-5 however many times to get the inches you need for the leg you are making it for. I did 15 times.
COF
Weave your chain into a braid, sew ends together, and you're done!!!

Booties

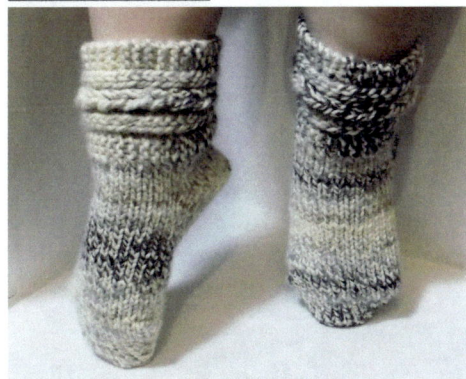

Video Tutorial Band: https://youtu.be/IIE_jQI0dBk
Video Tutorial: https://youtu.be/CbhTiye7JY8

Items:
30 peg 1/2" Gauge CinDwood Loom
Looming Hook
Crafters Needle
2 Skeins of Lions Brand Thick and Quick Wool Ease
Stitch Holder

Terms:
EW: E-Wrap
CO: Cast On
K: Flat Knit
P: Purl
SK: Skip
EWCH D-> BOLB: E-Wrap Chain, Decrease to the Right, Bring Original Loop Back on Empty Peg
COF: Cast Off
WCO: Weave In Cast On
KBO: Kitchener Bind Off

EWCO 18 pegs
Row 1: EW4, P1, EW2, P1, EW2, EW2, P1, EW4
Row 2: P4, P1, Sk2, P1, EW2, P1, Sk2, P1, P4
Row 3: K4, P1, EW2, P1, EW2, P1, EW2, P1, K4
Row 4: P4, P1, Sk2, P1, EWCH10 D-> BOLB, P1, Sk2, P1, P4
Row 5: K4, P1, EW2, P1, EW2, P1, EW2, P1, K4
Follow Rows 2-5 15 times. (Adult Sizing)
COF
Weave chain into braid, sew ends together, and add the last chain into seam.

WCO: Weave In Cast On: 
Start with the right side of the panel facing out, shove 1 end of the panel into the center of the loom. Send the crochet hook through the bridge between the 2 ridges at the top edge of your panel, grab the working yarn and pull through the bridge, place the loop on the peg. Continue the process of pulling the working yarn through the bridge between each secion, doing this all the way around till the top edge of the panel is attached to the loom.

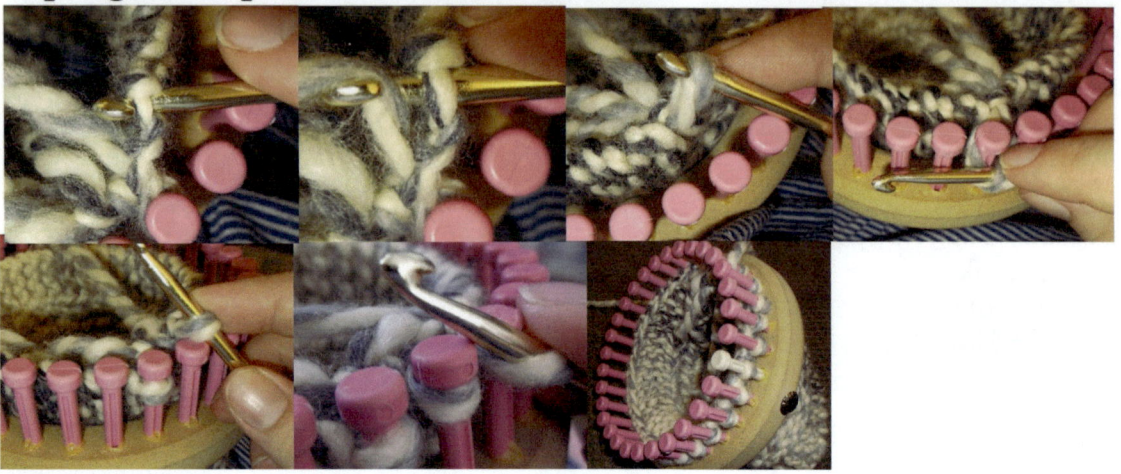

Bootie section
WCO 30pegs
Row 1-5: K
Row 6: K14, WT, K13, WT, K12, WT, K11, WT, K10, WT, K9, WT, K8, WT, K7, WT, K6, WT, K5, WT, K4, WT, K4, K5, K6, K7, K8, K9, K10, K11, K12, K13, K14, K30

Row 7-30: K

Row 31: Repeat row6

Row 32: K
KBO or COF and sew up toe.

Repeat for both booties.
To adjust for different size booties, follow my trace out method to accurate sizing. Example link provided below. Typically a 30peg loom is adult, 24 peg loom is small adult, 18 peg loom child, 14 peg loom toddler to baby. When keeping that in mind, and doing the small sizing for a toddler or child, remove some garter stitches on the end for the band to be thinner. https://www.youtube.com/watch?v=BD4p809eg9s

Cell Phone Case

Video Tutorial: https://youtu.be/IIE_jQI0dBk

Items:
30peg 1/2" gauge CinDwood Loom
Looming Hook
Crafters Needle
1 Skein of Lions Brand Thick and Quick Wool Ease Yarn
1 Button

Terms:
EW: E-Wrap
CO: Cast On
K: Flat Knit
P: Purl
SK: Skip
EWCH D-> BOLB: E-Wrap Chain, Decrease to the Right, Bring Original Loop Back on Empty Peg
COF: Cast Off

Basic Band Pattern:
EWCO 22 pegs
Row 1: EW6, P1, EW2, P1, EW2, P1, EW2, P1, EW6
Row 2: P6, P1, Sk2, P1, EW2, P1, Sk2, P1, P6
Row 3: K6, P1, EW2, P1, EW2, P1, EW2, P1, K6
Row 4: P6, P1, Sk2, P1, EWCH10 D-> BOLB, P1, Sk2, P1, P6
Row 5: K6, P1, EW2, P1, EW2, P1, EW2, P1, K6
Follow Rows 2-5 15times.
COF

Weave chain into braid, Fold a 3rd of the band up, and sew ends where it folds together. Sew on button on 3rd folded section, center top, use the last chain loop at the end or your braid as a button loop. If you have a larger, or longer phone, measure it, and adjust the length as needed. If it is longer, simply add extra stitches, to the garter stitch ends to add to the length for a longer phone. You're Done!!

Capelet

Video Tutorial Thin Band: https://youtu.be/IIE_jQI0dBk
Video Tutorial Large Band: https://youtu.be/6POpKiiJ0hg

Items:
60 peg 1/2" Gauge CinDwood Loom
Looming Hook
Crafters Needle
5 Skein of Lions Brand Thick and Quick Wool Ease
Measuring Tape

Terms:
EW: E-Wrap
CO: Cast On
K: Flat Knit
P: Purl
SK: Skip
EWCH D-> BOLB: E-Wrap Chain, Decrease to the Right, Bring Original Loop Back on Empty Peg.
COF: Cast Off

Hood
EWCO 60 pegs
Row 1: EW8, P1, EW2, P1, EW2, P1, EW2, P1, EW7, P1, EW2, P1, EW2, P1, EW2, P1, EW7, P1, EW2, P1, EW2, P1, EW2, P1, EW8
Row 2: P8, P1, SK2, P1, EW2, P1, SK2, P1, P7, P1, SK2, P1, EW2, P1, SK2, P1, P7, P1, SK2, P1, EW2, P1, SK2, P1, P8

Row 3: K8, P1, EW2, P1, EW2, P1, EW2, P1, K7, P1, EW2, P1, EW2, P1, EW2, P1, K7, P1, EW2, P1, EW2, P1, EW2, P1, K8
Row 4: P8, P1, SK2, P1, EWCH10 D-> BOLB, P1, SK2, P1, P7, P1, SK2, P1, EWCH10 D-> BOLB, P1, SK2, P1, P7, P1, SK2, P1, EWCH10 D-> BOLB, P1, SK2, P1, P8
Row 5: K8, P1, EW2, P1, EW2, P1, EW2, P1, K7, P1, EW2, P1, EW2, P1, EW2, P1, K7, P1, EW2, P1, EW2, P1, EW2, P1, K8
Repeat rows 2-5 15 times for child size, and 20 times for adult size. Cast off.
Chain your braid, fold the panel in half, where the braids will be vertical to the head, and will sew together at the top. There will be a back center braid, that follow the line down the back of the head.

Cape
EWCO 22 pegs
Row 1: EW6, P1, EW2, P1, EW2, P1, EW2, P1, EW6
Row 2: P6, P1, Sk2, P1, EW2, P1, Sk2, P1, P6
Row 3: K6, P1, EW2, P1, EW2, P1, EW2, P1, K6
Row 4: P6, P1, Sk2, P1, EWCH10 D-> BOLB, P1, Sk2, P1, P6
Row 5: K6, P1, EW2, P1, EW2, P1, EW2, P1, K6
Follow Rows 2-5 30 times for child size, 40 times for adult size.
COF
Chain your braid, sew the panel to the base of your hood. Tuck your ends, add a button at the connecting point of the bottom of the hood, and you're done!!!

Made in the USA
Columbia, SC
30 December 2023

29690468R00015